This or That

Questions
About
Space and Beyond

You Decide!

by Stephanie Bearce

CAPSTONE PRESS
a capstone imprint

Capstone Captivate is published by Capstone Press, an imprint of Capstone.
1710 Roe Crest Drive
North Mankato, Minnesota 56003
www.capstonepub.com

Library of Congress Cataloging-in-Publication Data
Names: Bearce, Stephanie, author.
Title: This or that questions about space and beyond : you decide! / by Stephanie Bearce.
Description: North Mankato, Minnesota : Capstone Press, [2021] | Series: This or that?: science edition | Includes bibliographical references and index. | Audience: Ages 8-11 | Audience: Grades 4-6 | Summary: "Space is full of mystery. Scientists think that the planets, stars, and other space objects we see make up just 4 percent of the universe! Scientists studying space have a lot of choices to make. Future space explorers will have many choices to consider too. Now the choices are yours. Would you rather eat pre-packaged space food or grow your own food in space? Would you rather catch a cold in space or have space sickness? Would you rather travel to Mars or Venus? It's your turn to pick this or that!"-- Provided by publisher.
Identifiers: LCCN 2020033111 (print) | LCCN 2020033112 (ebook) | ISBN 9781496695680 (hardcover) | ISBN 9781496696960 (paperback) | ISBN 9781977155115 (pdf) | ISBN 9781977156730 (kindle edition)
Subjects: LCSH: Outer space--Exploration--Miscellanea--Juvenile literature.
Classification: LCC QB500.262 .B43 2021 (print) | LCC QB500.262 (ebook) | DDC 520--dc23
LC record available at https://lccn.loc.gov/2020033111
LC ebook record available at https://lccn.loc.gov/2020033112

Image Credits
Getty Images: Chris Jackson, 13, Mark Wilson, 29; NASA: 17, JSC, 10, 12, 15, 18, 28, JSC/Roscosmos, 25, Kim Shiflett, 11; Shutterstock: 3Dsculptor, cover bottom right, 7, Alones, 21, Andrey Armyagov, 4–5, Artsiom Petrushenka, 8, Castleski, cover bottom left, clearviewstock, cover, 1, Corona Borealis Studio, 9, Dotted Yeti, 19, 26, FrameStockFootages, 16, GoodStudiode, design element, Monkey Business Images, 24, NASA images, 20, Nostalgia for Infinity, 6, 27, Paul Fleet, 23, Raymond Cassel, 22, Syda Productions, 14, Vadim Sadovski, cover top left, 3

Editorial Credits
Editor: Carrie Sheely; Designer: Sarah Bennett; Media Researcher: Tracy Cummins; Production Specialist: Spencer Rosio

All internet sites appearing in back matter were available and accurate when this book was sent to press.

Words in **bold** are in the glossary.

Printed and bound in China. 5934

Exploring the Mysteries of Space

Space is mysterious. People have explored very little of it. They are curious about what lies beyond Earth. Are there aliens living on other worlds? What are other **planets** like? People are discovering more **solar systems** every year. How many are out there?

Today, people use advanced tools such as **rovers** to explore planets. People have made plans for a space station on the moon, trips to Mars, and even space **colonies**.

But space exploration is very dangerous. Space station systems can fail. Lack of oxygen and extreme temperatures also make space a risky place. The choices explorers make can mean the difference between life and death.

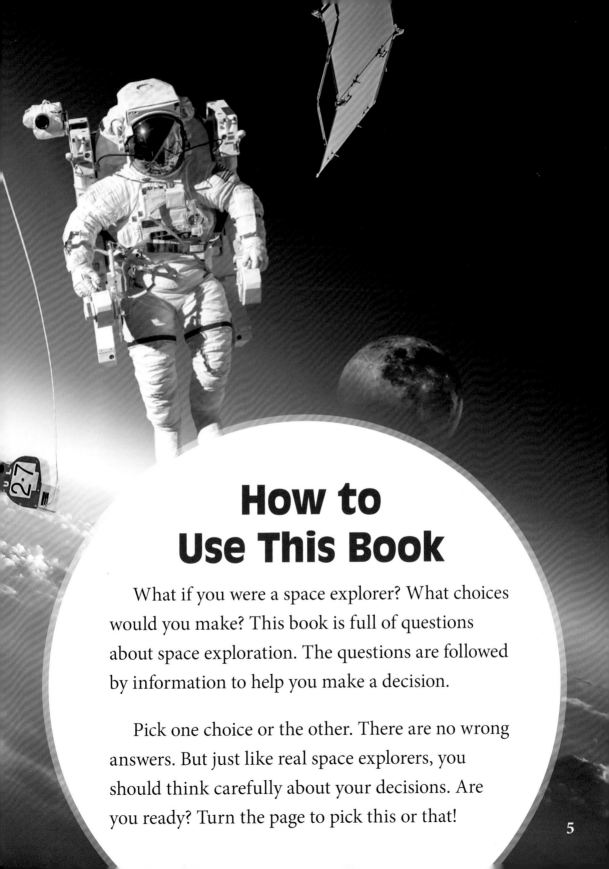

How to Use This Book

What if you were a space explorer? What choices would you make? This book is full of questions about space exploration. The questions are followed by information to help you make a decision.

Pick one choice or the other. There are no wrong answers. But just like real space explorers, you should think carefully about your decisions. Are you ready? Turn the page to pick this or that!

This

build a space station
that orbits the moon

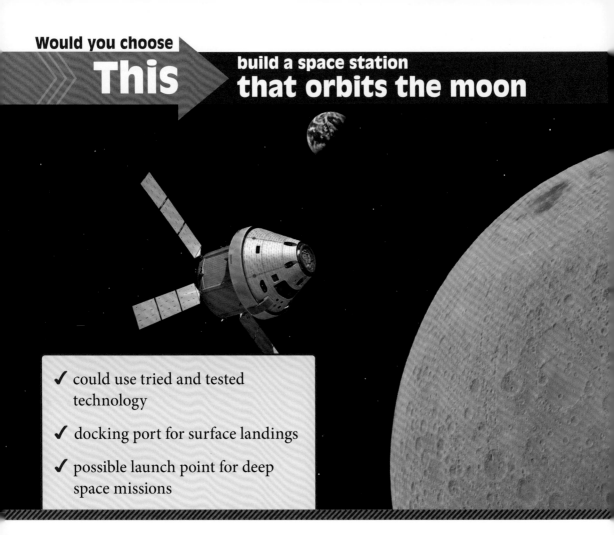

✓ could use tried and tested technology

✓ docking port for surface landings

✓ possible launch point for deep space missions

Some scientists want to build a space station that **orbits** the moon. The moon station they have planned would use a lot of proven **technology**. That would make it less expensive to build. The station would have a docking port. This would let the crew fly a lander to the moon. The port could also serve as a launch point to send spaceships into deep space.

✔ would use a lot of new technology

✔ very expensive

✔ could help build Mars colony

Some scientists want to build a station that orbits Mars. This would be expensive. The station would need to use new technology. For example, equipment would be needed to protect people from the sun's dangerous **radiation**. Unexpected problems could arise. It would take months to get help from Earth. But a Mars station would be a step to building a Mars colony.

This ➤ drive a moon buggy

✔ see the moon in person

✔ experience low gravity

✔ risk to life

Some astronauts who have visited the moon got to drive moon buggies. The small four-wheeled vehicles carry two astronauts. On the moon, astronauts experience low **gravity**. They feel lighter. They bounce. So do their buggies. It can be a thrilling experience. But it's dangerous. If the oxygen tank or other gear breaks, an astronaut can die.

✔ explore another world from the safety of Earth

✔ don't get to see space firsthand

✔ no risk to life

Mars is about 140 million miles (225 million kilometers) from Earth. The moon is about 238,000 miles (383,000 km) from Earth. Since Mars is far away, scientists send unmanned rovers to explore it. They use remote control to run the rovers. They can look at pictures from rovers. The pictures might help people make exciting discoveries. Sending rovers to space is also safer than sending people. No people have to risk their lives.

✔ food supplies must be regularly sent

✔ little preparation needed

✔ creates packaging waste

Astronauts eat prepackaged food in space. This food must be sent regularly to feed astronauts. It's easy for them to eat. For many foods, they just open the sealed bag, heat it, and eat. But they do have to save the trash until they can get rid of it properly. Packaged food also can be less flavorful than fresh food.

OR
That?
grow your own
food in space

✓ requires large area

✓ reduces transportation costs

✓ fresh food is available

Some astronauts are learning to grow vegetables in space. This allows them to have fresh food. Astronauts grow plants with very little soil and water. The work may lead to a long-term food source in space. Then less food would need to be brought from Earth. This could reduce costs. But growing food takes up a lot of room on a space station.

- ✓ water floats everywhere
- ✓ need airflow system
- ✓ escaping droplets can cause problems with electronics

Keeping clean in space is not as easy as it is on Earth. Astronauts squeeze liquid soap from pouches onto their skin. They rinse off with a pouch of water and dry their skin with a towel. They use an airflow system to suck up the extra water. But droplets can escape and float all over. This can cause problems with station electronics.

✔ need to use special tools

✔ suction necessary

✔ pee can escape

Using the toilet in space is tricky. On Earth, you can depend on gravity to pull poop and pee away from your body. But in space, they float. Space toilets use air suction to pull waste away from the astronaut and into the tank. The system works most of the time. But pee droplets do sometimes escape and float around.

This ▸ catch a cold in space

- ✔ need to catch sneezes quickly in tissues
- ✔ can spread germs easily to others
- ✔ ear canals and sinuses get clogged

Sneezing in space is like a snot explosion. The saliva and mucus fly everywhere. Astronauts try to catch their sneezes with tissues, but not every drop gets caught. The germs float and can infect others. In space, people's ear canals and sinuses don't drain properly. Astronauts report feeling worse when they have a cold in space than on Earth.

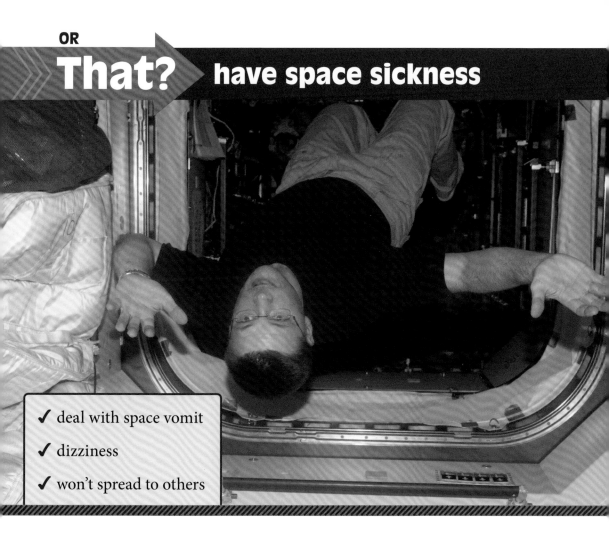

✔ deal with space vomit

✔ dizziness

✔ won't spread to others

In low gravity, the fluids inside the human body float. This confuses the inner ear and makes it hard for the body to know up from down. The floating fluids cause motion sickness. It makes people feel dizzy. It can also make them throw up. Every astronaut is given a "barf bag." It is important to vomit in the bag. Otherwise, vomit will float. The good news is that space sickness can't spread to others.

This

cryosleep
for a trip to distant planets

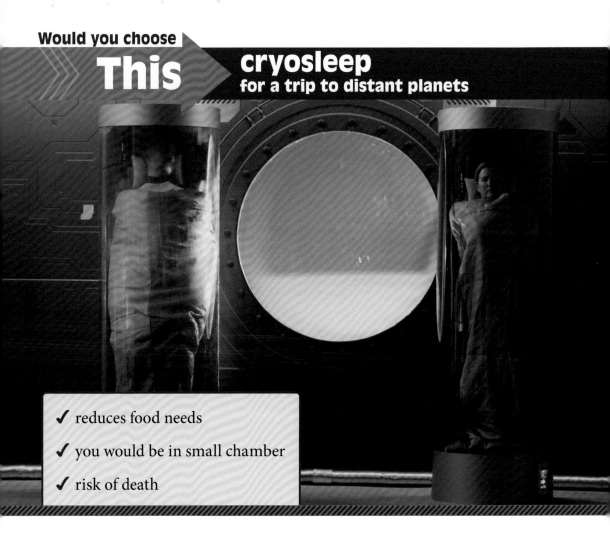

✔ reduces food needs

✔ you would be in small chamber

✔ risk of death

It can take months or years to reach faraway planets. Scientists think cryosleep might work for space travelers someday. Cryosleep is like deep hibernation. It would lower the body's temperature and put it to sleep. The astronaut would sleep in a small chamber. Food and water would be given through the veins. This would reduce the amount of food necessary. But if something goes wrong in the chamber, the astronaut could die.

✔ able to work

✔ can adjust to life in space

✔ need more food

Staying awake for the whole trip to a faraway planet would allow astronauts to work. They could do experiments and solve problems. It also would help them adjust to life in space. But astronauts would need a lot of food. Extra supplies increase the spacecraft's weight and take up a lot of room.

✔ can cause health problems

✔ need time to get used to low gravity

✔ limits crews to short-term missions

On a space station, people float. They feel weightless. It makes space life new and interesting. But people need time to get used to this way of life. Weightlessness also comes at a cost. Muscles get weak. Bones can easily break. Astronauts risk their health on long space missions.

- ✓ healthier for astronauts
- ✓ need large station
- ✓ would allow for long-term missions

Scientists believe that a spinning space station could be built. It would create gravity for space travelers using **centrifugal force**. The spinning motion would force the feet to stay on the ground. People's bones and muscles would stay healthy. But the station would need to be large. A great deal of time and money would be needed to build it.

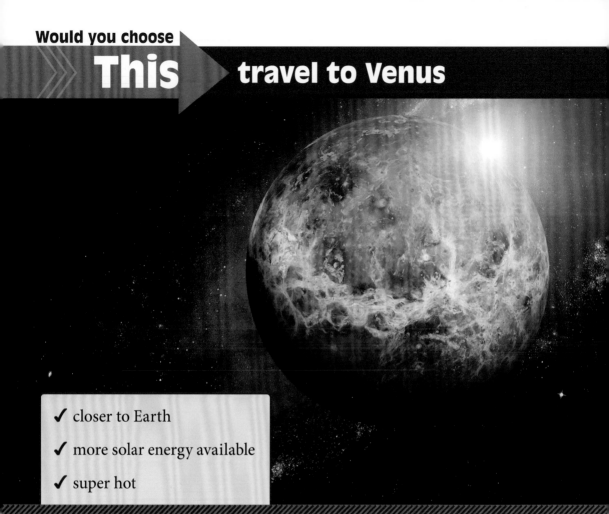

✔ closer to Earth

✔ more solar energy available

✔ super hot

Venus is the planet closest to Earth. It is about 25 million miles (40 million km) away. A trip to Venus would take about 110 days. The planet gets a lot of sunlight. People could use solar energy to power machines. But the planet's surface is more than 800 degrees Fahrenheit (400 degrees Celsius). People can't survive there. Instead, scientists think astronauts could live in the planet's thick **atmosphere** in a floating space station.

That? travel to Mars

✓ farther from Earth

✓ little solar energy

✓ cold

Mars is about 140 million miles (225 million km) from Earth. It would take about seven months to get there. Mars is cold, but temperatures can be tolerable near its middle. Heat and water would have to be pumped in to shelters. Mars gets less solar energy than Earth. Different power sources would be needed. It also has less gravity than Earth. This could cause health problems for people on long stays.

This ▶ mine asteroids
for minerals

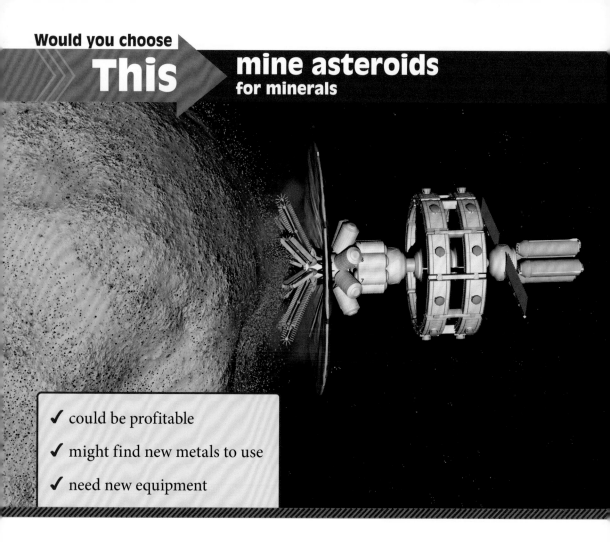

- ✔ could be profitable
- ✔ might find new metals to use
- ✔ need new equipment

Asteroids are rocks that orbit the sun. Many are full of precious minerals such as gold and silver. Scientists think people might be able to mine asteroids someday. They could make a lot of money selling the minerals. Mining asteroids could also provide new metals for technology. But the process would require new mining equipment to be made.

That?

mine Mars
for water

✔ provides a basic need for human life

✔ might help support a space colony

✔ possible to use tools available on Earth

Mars has frozen water under the surface. This water is important for building a colony. Mining teams could drill and take out the ice. It could be melted and used. This would help a colony grow. Research has shown the water is near the surface. Some of the drilling tools could be like those used on Earth.

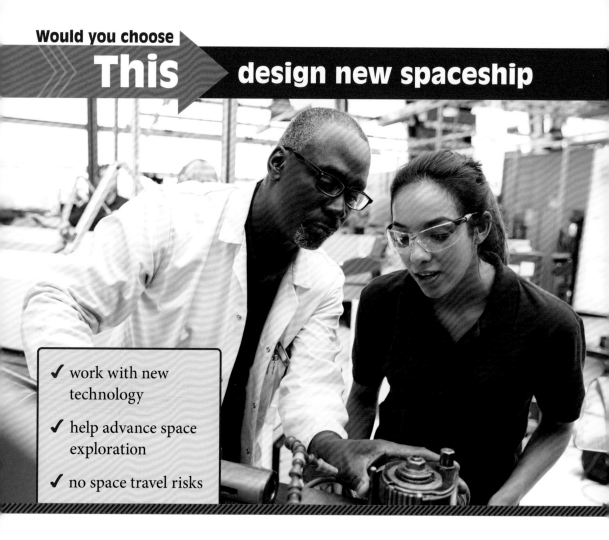

- ✓ work with new technology
- ✓ help advance space exploration
- ✓ no space travel risks

Engineers work to create new designs for better spaceships. They research new fuels. They test new metals. They invent new safety gear. Engineers make **computer models** of the ships before they are built to check their designs. After they are built, designers do testing. Their work helps advance space exploration.

✓ train for years

✓ lead team of astronauts

✓ responsible for crew safety

Mission commanders are in charge of space crews. They have years of experience in space flight. Commanders assign jobs. They supervise research. If something goes wrong, the commander must fix the problem. Mistakes can put the lives of all crew members at risk.

This colonize Titan

- ✓ cold
- ✓ standing bodies of liquid
- ✓ radiation protection

Titan is one of Saturn's icy moons. Its atmosphere is thick. This would provide protection from radiation. Titan has standing bodies of liquid. This liquid is methane and ethane. People might be able to burn methane for fuel. Scientists think Titan has an ocean under the ice. People might be able to drill down and use the water. But like Europa, Titan is cold. Protection from the weather would be needed.

- ✓ cold
- ✓ little radiation protection
- ✓ might require underwater living

Europa is an ice moon of Jupiter. Its surface has many long cracks. It is freezing cold. The atmosphere is thin. There wouldn't be enough radiation protection. People might be forced to live under the ice sheet for radiation protection. A liquid ocean is under the ice. Some scientists think this water might be warmer than the moon's surface. But living underwater requires technology that allows people to breathe and get food and drinking water.

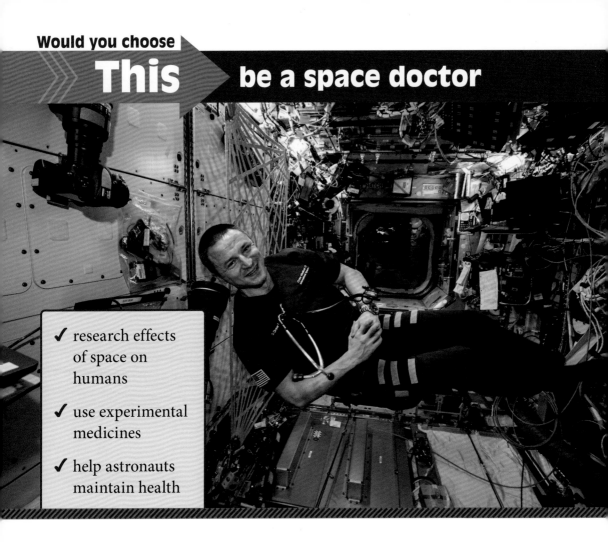

- ✓ research effects of space on humans
- ✓ use experimental medicines
- ✓ help astronauts maintain health

Space doctors help astronauts stay healthy. They keep track of a crew's exercise and diet. They give astronauts vitamins and medicine. The doctors research how low gravity affects people. They create exercise machines for space stations. They also help design space suits. Some doctors even travel into space with astronauts.

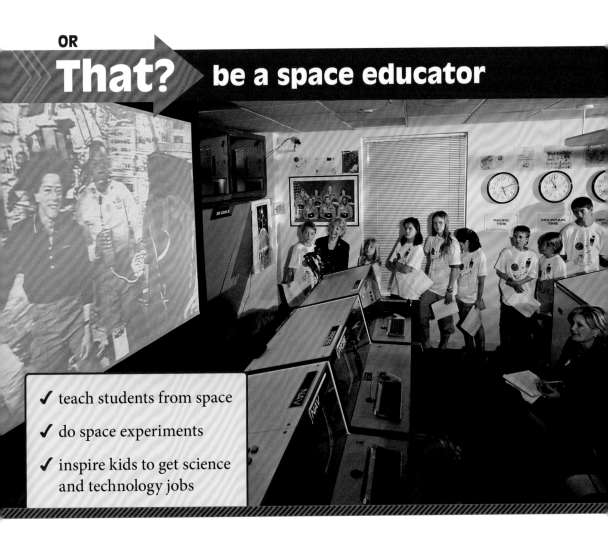

OR That? be a space educator

✓ teach students from space

✓ do space experiments

✓ inspire kids to get science and technology jobs

Space educators travel with astronauts. They help students learn about space exploration. They do experiments and teach classes from space stations. Their job is to get kids interested in science and technology. This could inspire students to pursue space-related careers.

Lightning Round

Would you choose to . . .

➡ travel to a planet that scientists know a lot about **or** to one they know little about?

➡ take a dog **or** a robot with you to Mars?

➡ experiment with plants **or** squid on a space station?

➡ exercise on a space cycle **or** do space weight lifting?

➡ take out space garbage **or** vacuum a space station?

➡ name a new planet **or** discover a new star?

➡ repair the outside of a space station **or** the space toilet?

Glossary

atmosphere (AT-muhss-fihr)—a blanket of gases that surrounds a planet

centrifugal force (sen-TRI-fyuh-guhl FORS)—the physical force that causes a body rotating around a center to move away from the center

colony (KAH-luh-nee)—a place that is settled by people from another country or planet

computer model (kuhm-PYOO-tuhr MOD-uhl)—a design of something on a computer; computer models can help people see how a new machine or invention will work

gravity (GRAV-uh-tee)—the force of attraction between two objects; for example, the sun's gravity holds Earth and the other planets in orbit around it

orbit (OR-bit)—to travel around an object in space

planet (PLAN-it)—a large object that orbits a star

radiation (ray-dee-AY-shuhn)—rays of energy given off by certain elements; radiation can harm people

rover (ROH-vur)—a vehicle that people can move by using remote control; rovers are used to explore objects in space

solar system (SOH-lur SISS-tuhm)—a sun and all the planets, moons, comets, and smaller bodies orbiting it

technology (tek-NAHL-uh-jee)—the use of science to do practical things

Read More

Clay, Kathryn. *Living in Space*. North Mankato, MN: Capstone Press, 2017.

Collins, Ailynn. *Mars or Bust!: Orion and the Mission to Deep Space*. North Mankato, MN: Capstone Press, 2020.

Gregory, Josh. *If You Were a Kid Docking at the International Space Station*. New York: Children's Press, an imprint of Scholastic Inc., 2018.

Internet Sites

ESA Kids
www.esa.int/kids/en/home

NASA: Mars Exploration
mars.nasa.gov/participate/funzone/

Space.com: Europa: Facts About Jupiter's Icy Moon and Its Ocean
www.space.com/15498-europa-sdcmp.html